The Quest for Speed
Vehicles

Lisa Greathouse

The Quest for Speed
Vehicles

Publishing Credits

Editorial Director
Dona Herweck Rice

Associate Editors
James Anderson
Torrey Maloof

Editor-in-Chief
Sharon Coan, M.S.Ed.

Creative Director
Lee Aucoin

Illustration Manager
Timothy J. Bradley

Publisher
Rachelle Cracchiolo, M.S.Ed.

Science Consultant
Scot Oschman, Ph.D.

Teacher Created Materials
5301 Oceanus Drive
Huntington Beach, CA 92649-1030
http://www.tcmpub.com

ISBN 978-1-4333-0305-0

Printed by: 51497
Printed in: China

Table of Contents

Getting From One Place to Another—*Fast!*

Humans are always looking for ways to travel faster. Everyone wants to get from one place to another in less time.

Our vehicles (VEE-uh-kuhls) have changed a lot over the years. Hundreds of years ago, people traveled in wagons pulled by horses. In the 1800s, you could travel to some places by train and steamboat. In the early 1900s, the car was invented. This made traveling much easier. Then people began traveling by airplane. They were able to get across the country in hours instead of days.

1807

first steam boat

1885

early motorcycle

1885

early automobile

Some people prefer vehicles they power themselves. These include bikes, scooters, and skates.

And then there are people who not only want to be fast—they want to be the *fastest*. They like the idea of setting records for going faster than anyone else. They might be race car drivers, pilots, cyclists—or snowmobilers! These are the people who strive for speed.

1903

Wright Brothers and an early airplane

1981

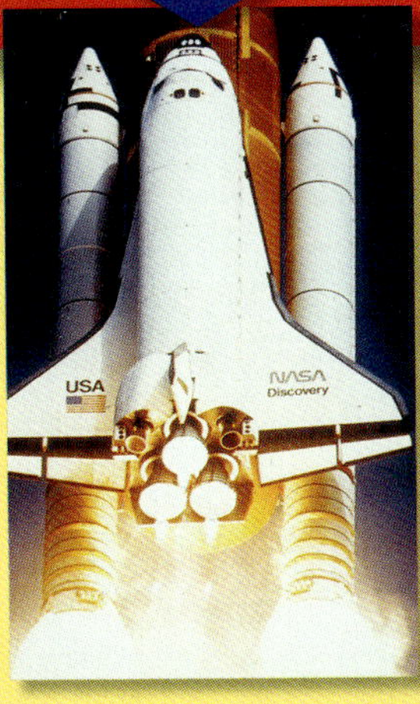

first space shuttle flight

2004

first private, manned space flight, *SpaceShipOne*

Always Moving

Whether something is going fast or slow, **motion** is always involved. Motion is how, where, and why something moves.

Everything in the universe moves. You might be standing still, but the Earth moves around the sun. That means everything on Earth is moving. Stars and planets move. The vehicles that take you places *definitely* move!

But nothing moves on its own. For an object to move, **force** is needed. This involves a push or pull. Forces can make objects speed up, slow down, or change direction. Think about pushing your foot on your bicycle's pedal. You are applying force to an object to make it move!

The amount of force that is needed to move something depends on the object's **mass**. Mass is the amount of "stuff"—or matter—that makes up the object. It would take more force to move a bike that has two people on it than a bike that has just one person on it.

That Weightless Feeling

A spaceship in orbit is falling slowly to Earth. Since the ship and the astronauts are falling at the same speed, the astronauts do not press against anything. They feel weightless.

Hardly Moving

Even in a traffic jam, people are still moving. Since Earth is constantly rotating and orbiting the sun, that means *we* are moving, too.

A Force of Nature

Isaac Newton lived in the 1600s. He is one of the most famous scientists in history. He used math to describe forces he saw in nature. The math used today to figure out how things move is named after him. It is called Newtonian Mechanics.

Newton's Laws of Motion

Isaac Newton studied motion. His work led to laws about the way things move. The first law says that an object at rest will stay at rest if there is no outside force to put it in motion. It also says that a moving object will keep moving at the same speed and in the same direction unless something gets in the way. That is called **momentum** (moh-MEN-tuhm).

Have you ever wondered why you need to wear a seat belt while riding in a car? Look no further than Newton's Laws of Motion. You have probably been in a car when it stopped suddenly. Even if you were wearing a seat belt, you may have felt your body jerk forward when the driver slammed on the brakes. In this situation, your body was moving at the same speed as the car. When the car stopped suddenly, your body kept moving in the same direction. The seat belt stopped you from flying out of your seat. Seat belts save thousands of lives every year.

Buckle Up

Safety experts agree that buckling up makes it much more likely that you will be safe in an accident.

More Laws of Motion

Newton's second law explains what happens when you apply a force to an object. The object speeds up or slows down. The greater the force, the more the object speeds up or slows down.

When you pedal your bike, you create force. The harder you pedal, the faster the bike moves forward.

Newton's third law says that when a force pushes on an object, something will happen in response to that force. The object pushes back in the opposite direction. Imagine if you and a friend were both on roller blades. If you gave your friend a push forward, what would happen? You would not stand still. You would roll backward. That is Newton's third law of motion.

Newton's Laws of Motion

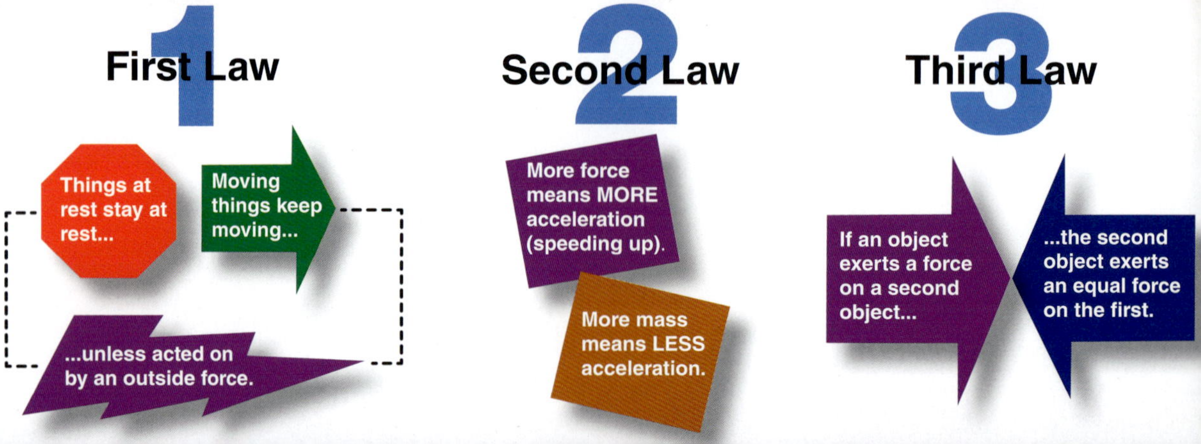

Defying Gravity

Do you remember learning how to ride a bike? You probably fell down a lot at first. To keep the bike moving forward, you have to make the wheels go fast. If you do not, **gravity** pulls you down. When you get the wheels going fast, they create an anti-gravity force. So, when you ride your bike, you are defying gravity!

Measuring Motion

So how do we measure all this motion? Scientists and **engineers** (en-juh-NEERS) need to measure motion to make sure the vehicles we use are safe. But anyone who drives a car, boat, plane, or motorcycle also needs to know how fast the vehicle is going. There are laws that tell us how fast—or how slow—we can safely go.

There are many ways to measure an object's motion. Distance, direction, and speed are some of the ways. Speed is how far something moves in a given time. If your car is going 72 kilometers (45 miles) per hour, in 60 minutes the car would have traveled 72 kilometers (45 miles) from where it started. Every motor vehicle has a **speedometer** (spee-DOM-uh-ter). It tells the rate at which the vehicle is moving.

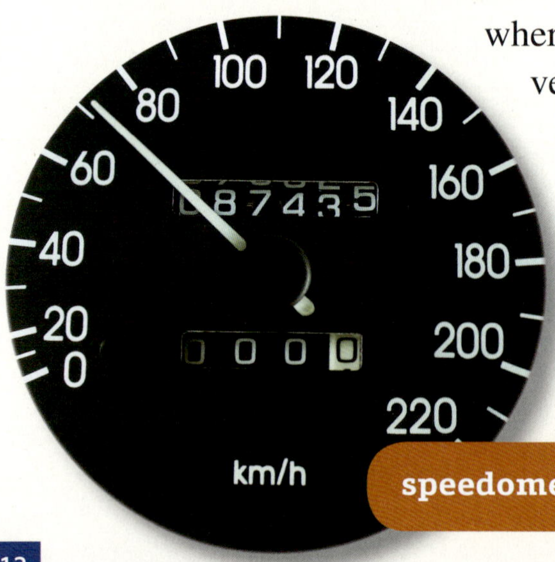

speedometer

A Different Kind of Knot

If you are on a boat, you would use nautical miles to measure the distance you travel. Nautical miles are also called knots. Sailors used to measure boat speed by tossing the end of a knotted rope overboard. As more rope was pulled into the water, they would count how many knots went by. Each knot was equal to one nautical mile.

Comparing Distances

1 nautical mile per hour =
1.85 kilometers per hour
or
1.15 miles per hour

Velocity and Acceleration

Velocity (vuh-LOS-uh-tee) tells us how an object's position changes over time. It is a change in speed *and* direction. Think about an exercise bicycle. You might be pedaling very fast. But you do not change position. So there is zero velocity.

Another measurement is **acceleration**. (ak-sel-uh-RAY-shuhn). Acceleration means more than just moving fast. An object is accelerating if it is changing speed. Think of a parked car. When it starts moving forward, it is accelerating. When it slows down, it is negative acceleration. That is called **deceleration** (dee-sel-uh-RAY-shuhn).

SpaceShipOne

Concorde

Thrust SSC

the SR-71 Blackbird

Colonel Walter L. Watson, Jr.

Colonel Watson was the first African American to qualify as a crew member for the SR-71. This secret Air Force plane still holds altitude and speed records

See Space for Yourself

In 2004, pilot Mike Melvill made history. He piloted *SpaceShipOne* into Earth's orbit. But he is not an astronaut. This gave hope to millions of people who dream about going to space. Scientists are looking for ways to make space travel faster and less costly. Maybe one day, it will be your turn to rocket into space!

Which Plane Is Fastest?

One of the fastest planes ever built was the *Concorde*. The supersonic jetliner flew at 2,180 kilometers (1,354 miles) per hour. It cut the time to get from New York to Paris in half, from seven hours to just three and one-half hours. The plane stopped flying in 2003 due to high costs. Faster planes are being planned for the future!

Which Land Vehicle Is Fastest?

The *Thrust SSC* holds the title of fastest land vehicle. It set the first supersonic land speed record with a speed of 1,228 kilometers (763 miles) per hour. The record was set by Andy Green in Nevada in 1997. The team that designed the vehicle is currently designing a new model called the *Bloodhound SSC*, which is expected to reach speeds above 1,609 kilometers (1,000 miles) per hour!

Moving Machines

You may not think of your car as a **machine**. But that is exactly what it is. Machines make it easier for people to do work. The car that takes you to school or to the store is making it easier for you to get from one place to another.

The car's engine applies a force to turn its wheels. That makes the car move. But all machines need a source of **energy** to make them work. On a bicycle or skateboard, your body movements create energy. In the case of a car—or anything with an engine —that energy is fuel.

Alternative Fuels

Most personal vehicles (cars and light trucks) use gasoline. But many vehicles today are running on cleaner fuels that are better for the environment. Some vehicles run on electricity, natural gas, propane, or ethanol. Hybrid vehicles use electricity *and* gasoline. They can go much farther on a tank of gas than a car that uses gasoline alone.

New technology is creating vehicles that run farther on less fuel. They are better for the environment, too!

Fossil Fuels

Most of our vehicles use fossil fuels. The three main types are coal, oil, or petroleum, and natural gas. We get this energy mostly by digging it out of the ground. It comes from the remains of tiny plants and animals that lived millions of years ago. But the problem is that fossil fuels cause pollution. They damage Earth and its atmosphere. Also, our supplies are running low. Scientists are searching for other forms of energy.

Machines such as these pump fossil fuels from the ground.

How Does a Car Move?

Have you ever looked under the hood of a car? It is hard to figure out how all of those twisted wires and tubes get you from one place to another.

When you start a car's engine, it burns gasoline to create motion. Then some new forces come into play. The rear wheels create a force against the ground. That pushes the car forward. Air creates a force *against* the car. The faster the car goes, the stronger the force of air against it. The way the air flows around a moving object is called **aerodynamics** (air-oh-dye-NAM-iks). The way a car is designed can change how well it moves through the air.

gasoline engine

Another force that can slow you down is **friction** (FRIK-shuhn). There is friction whenever objects come into contact with one another. Friction is what slows you down when you come to a stop sign. First, the driver steps on the brake pedal. The friction between the brakes and the wheels slows the car down. If you are riding a skateboard and you want to stop, you would put a foot on the ground. You can stop because of the friction between your shoe and the cement.

When Friction Helps Us

Drivers need to take special care when roads are wet. Slippery roads mean less friction. It is much easier for tires to grip the road when it is dry. Cars may skid when the road is wet. Many vehicles are equipped with special brakes that help drivers avoid skids.

Cars With Wings

Have you ever noticed something that looks like a wing on the back of a car? This is called a spoiler. They make cars more aerodynamic and more stable on the road.

Types of Boats

steamboat

cargo boat

speed boat

cruise liner

Types of Trains

steam locomotive

Amtrak train

maglev train

Speeding Up Travel

Humans have always tried to figure out how to get from one place to another faster. Famous artist Leonardo da Vinci was sketching flying machines in the 1400s! That was hundreds of years before a steam engine was first used in a boat in 1807. Today, some boats are built for speed. Power speedboats can go over 160 kilometers (100 miles) per hour. A cruise liner might only travel about 40 kilometers (25 miles) per hour. But it is carrying thousands of people.

The steam engine was also used in trains. The steam locomotive [low-co-MOW-tive] carried goods and people over long distances. From the mid-1800s to the early 1900s, it was the way most people traveled. Many people still take the train today. But today's trains are much faster. Most have diesel (DEE-suhl) engines or run on electricity. Some new trains travel up to 500 kilometers (310 miles) per hour!

Maglev Trains

Right now, the fastest way to travel long distances is by air. But a few countries have developed high-speed trains. Maglev stands for magnetic levitation. Maglev trains use powerful electromagnets to float above the tracks. This allows maglev trains to travel at top speeds.

We Love Our Cars!

You might wonder how people ever got around without a car. The first car powered by gasoline was invented in 1896. At first, only wealthy people could afford cars. But it was not long before most families owned cars. These early cars could only go about 16 kilometers (10 miles) per hour.

Today, millions of people drive cars and trucks every day. Freeways continue to grow to allow more cars on the road. People love cars because they are fast, comfortable, fun to drive, and people can go almost anywhere in them. Most cars can go over 160 kilometers (100 miles) per hour. But it is dangerous to go that fast. So, there are speed-limit laws. How fast you can go depends on where you are. If you are driving on a street with a school, you must drive very slowly. If you are on a freeway, you can drive faster.

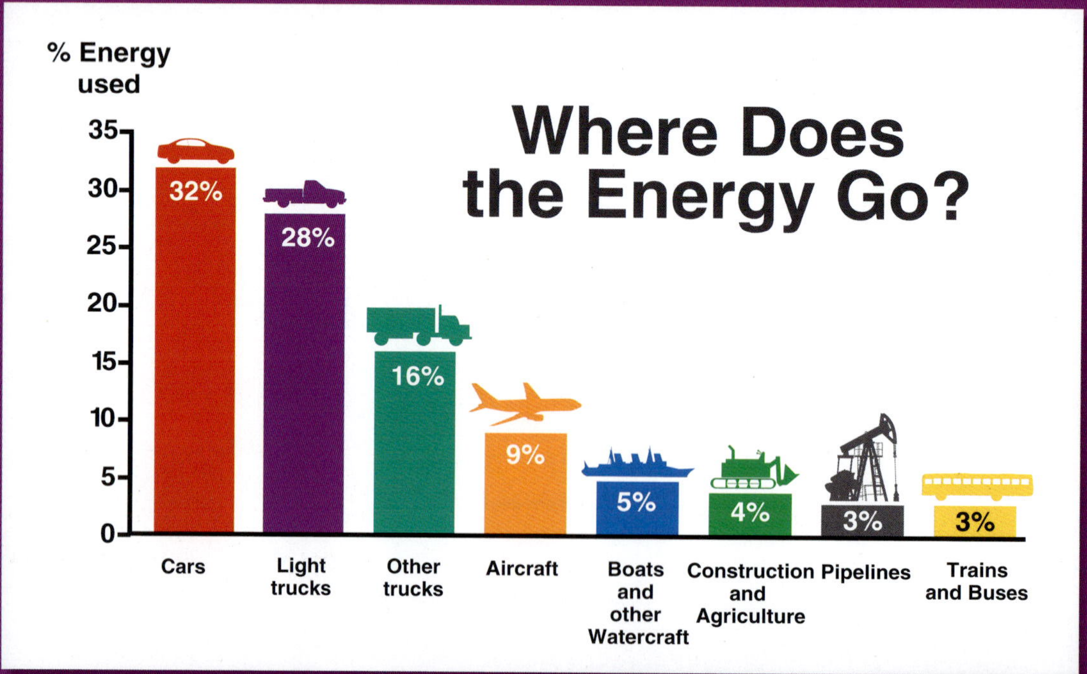

Always on the Move

There are about 240 million vehicles (cars, buses, and trucks) in the United States. That is more than three motor vehicles for every four people!

The earliest cars looked a lot like carriages that were pulled by horses. They became known as "horseless carriages."

Taking Wing

At the same time the first cars were being built, two brothers were building the first airplane. Orville and Wilbur Wright took the first successful flight in 1903. That flight was just 12 seconds long.

the Wright brothers' first plane

In the years that followed, bigger and faster planes were built for the military. Jet airliners started to transport people in the 1950s. Today, jumbo jets fly more than 800 kilometers (500 miles) per hour. The fastest jets can travel seven times the **speed of sound**.

Future of Space Flight

In 1969, Neil Armstrong became the first human to step on the moon. That was just 66 years after the Wright brothers took their first flight. In 2006, **NASA** launched its fastest spacecraft to date. *New Horizons* is on a mission to Pluto. It travels 80,470 kilometers (50,000 miles) per hour! In just about 100 years, the science of flight has come a long way.

The cloud of vapor is a sign of a sonic boom.

Speed of Sound

Sound is made by vibrations in the air that travel at about 1,200 kilometers (760 miles) per hour. The speed of sound is called Mach (mahk) 1. When an airplane travels this fast, you hear a sonic boom.

Force in the Air

Aerodynamics is the study of forces and the resulting motion of objects through the air. Aerodynamics affects everything that moves in the air. Jet airliners, kites, and model rockets are all examples of things affected by aerodynamics. The curveball thrown by a baseball pitcher gets its curve from aerodynamics.

***New Horizons* launching**

History of Racing

Auto racing is one of the most popular sports in the world. The first race was held in 1895. Most racetracks are oval in shape. The sport is divided into different types of racing. They include stock-car racing, open-wheel racing, and Formula One racing.

Formula One racers (above) and racecar driver in safety gear (left)

Being Safe at Any Speed

Almost everyone loves to go fast. It is exciting. And it gets you to where you are going in less time. Almost every new vehicle boasts faster speeds. It is why a lot of people want the latest car, scooter, or even private jet.

But more speed means more risk. The faster a car is moving, the more danger there is for everyone involved if there is a crash. The faster you are riding a scooter, the more risk you are taking if you should hit a bump and fall off. Racecar drivers always want to go faster, but they also wear the latest safety gear. Seat belts are a must in cars. And you need to wear helmets and other safety gear when you are riding on personal vehicles. Safety is always more important than speed!

Speed Limits

There are only a few places in the world that do not have speed limits on their roads. In Germany, most of the motorway system has no speed limit. In the United States, many highways have a speed limit of 105 kilometers (65 miles) per hour. The highest posted speed limit in the world is 160 kilometers (99 miles) per hour. That is in Austria and the United Arab Emirates.

Lab: Seat Belt Safety

When riding in a car, you are moving at the same speed as the car. It is important to wear your seat belt! If the car has to stop suddenly, the seat belt will keep you from flying out of your seat.

Materials

- piece of stiff cardboard, at least 45 cm x 30 cm (18 inches x 12 inches)
- two books, each about 2.5 cm (1 inch) thick
- masking tape
- pencil
- piece of modeling clay
- small toy car
- piece of ribbon, 30 cm (12 inches) long
- ruler
- stopwatch

Procedure:

1. Take the piece of cardboard and place one end of it on the edge of one of the books, creating a ramp.
2. Tape the other end of the cardboard to a table or onto the floor.
3. Tape the pencil to the table about two toy-car lengths from the taped end of the cardboard.
4. Use the clay to make a small figure, such as a snowman, about 5 centimeters (2 inches) tall.

5. Flatten the bottom of the clay figure and rest it on the car's hood. Do not press the clay onto the car.
6. Position the car and clay figure at the raised end of the cardboard.
7. At the same time you release the car to roll down the cardboard, start the stopwatch. Stop the stopwatch when the car hits the pencil. Record the time. Also record how many inches the clay figure lands from the pencil. Use a table like the one shown below.
8. Use the ribbon to tie the clay figure to the car. Then repeat steps five through seven. The clay figure should stay on the car.
9. Now, stack two books instead of one under the cardboard to make the ramp steeper. Repeat the experiment.
10. Compare the times and distances. Why are the distances and times different?

	One–Book Ramp	**Two–Book Ramp**
Car Speed (with loose clay figure, in seconds)		
Car Speed (with tied-on clay figure, in seconds)		
Clay Figure Landing (inches from pencil)		

Glossary

acceleration—a change in speed

aerodynamics—the study of the movement of air

deceleration—a reduction in speed

energy—the power to do work

engineer—a person who plans, builds, or manages a project

force—a push or pull that makes things move

friction—a force that acts on surfaces in contact and slows them down

gravity—a force that attracts things to each other

machine—something that uses one movement to make work easier

mass—the amount of matter something is made of

momentum—the force or speed of movement

motion—a change in position

NASA—National Aeronautics and Space Administration

speed of sound—vibrations in the air that are made by sound and travel at about 1,200 kilometers (760 miles) per hour

speedometer—a gauge that tells the rate at which a vehicle is moving

velocity—the rate of change of position

Index

Scientists Then and Now

Wernher von Braun
(1912–1977)

Human beings are forever on a quest to excel. Wernher von Braun was no exception. He was born in Germany and became a leading figure in the development of rockets. He helped to develop rockets for America's space program. He was the chief engineer for the *Saturn V* rocket that propelled the *Apollo* spacecraft to the moon. He was also a big part of getting public support for the whole space program.

Ron Ayers
(1932–)

In school in England, Ron Ayers studied planes, spaceships, and flight. After college, he worked to help make airplanes and missiles fly better. Eventually, he retired from his job. But he was still curious. He studied more about flight and speed. Then he worked with a group of people to break the sound barrier with a land vehicle. It was the fastest land vehicle ever at 1,228 kilometers (763 miles) per hour!

Image Credits

Cover Sergei Bachlakov/Shutterstock; p.1 Sergei Bachlakov/Shutterstock; p.4(left) Library of Congress; p.4(middle) Library of Congress; p.4(right) Library of Congress; p.5(left) The Granger Collection, New York; p.5(middle) NASA; p.5(right) Courtesy of Derek Webber; p.5(top) Jupiterimages Corporation; p.6-7(bottom) Jeremy Woodhouse/Blend Images/Corbis; p.6-7(top) NASA; p.7 egd/Shutterstock; p.8 The Granger Collection, New York; p.9 sonya etchison/Shutterstock; p.10-11 Jupiterimages Corporation; p.11 greenland/Shutterstock; p.12 Adrian Lucki/Shutterstock; p.12-13 James Cavallini/Photo Researchers, Inc.; p.12-13(top) Bruce Amos/Shutterstock; p.14(left) Suzanne Tucker/Shutterstock; .14-15(top) NASA; p.14-15(top middle) ROBYN BECK/AFP/Getty Images/Newscom; p.14-15(bottom middle) AFP PHOTO/FILES/Newcsom; p.14-15(bottom) Yousef Allan/AP Photo; p.16 maigi/Shutterstock; p.17 zhuda/Shutterstock; p.18-19(top) Transtock Inc./Alamy; p.18-19 Oleksiy Maksymenko/Alamy; p.19 Daniela Mangiuca/Shutterstock; p.20(top left) Library of Congress; p.20(upper middle left) Olivier Le Queinec/Shutterstock; p.20(lower middle left) Zdorov Kirill Vladimirovich/Shutterstock; p.20(bottom left) Ivan Cholakov/Shutterstock; p.20(top right) Nik Niklz/Shutterstock; p.20(middle right) Amtrak/Dallas Morning News/KRT/Newscom; p.20(bottom right) Lee Prince/Shutterstock; p.21 Stephanie Reid; p.22-23 Newscom; p.24(top) John Daniels/UPI Photo/Newscom; p.24(bottom) PHOTO USN via ABACA/Newscom; p.24-25 BRUCE WEAVER/AFP/Getty Images/Newscom; p.26 JOSEP LAGO/AFP/Getty Images; p.26-27 Sergei Bachlakov/Shutterstock; p.28 jaddingt/Shutterstock; p.29 Eimantas Buzas/Shutterstock; p.32(left) NASA; p.32(right) Rick Reason